GW00585239

EXETER AND TAUNTON TRAMWAYS

J B Perkin

Series editor **Robert J Harley**

MP Middleton Press

First published May 1994

ISBN 1 873793 32 4

© Middleton Press 1994

Design - Deborah Goodridge

Published by Middleton Press
            Easebourne Lane
            Midhurst
            West Sussex
            GU29 9AZ
            Tel: (0730) 813169
(From 16 April 1995 - (01730) 813169)

Printed & bound by Biddles Ltd,
            Guildford and Kings Lynn

Exeter Tramways 1-70
Taunton Tramways 71-120

INTRODUCTION AND ACKNOWLEDGEMENTS

In January 1992 I was requested by Peter Lindsay of the Exe Model Railway Society to arrange an exhibition of Exeter tramways for their annual show in June of that year. Using the experience gained in collecting information for Taunton, I rapidly gathered together photographs, drawings and photocopies of memorabilia of the horse and electric tramways of Exeter.

Special mention should be made of the work of G.N. Southerden (1905-1943), a native of Exeter, whose views are used extensively in the following pages. The National Tramway Museum library has also supplied many valuable views. Tickets were made available by G.Croughton.

Permission to reproduce car drawings has been kindly given by T.M.Russell and J.C. Gillham has similarly allowed the use of his maps. Great assistance on aspects of Exeter has been received from G.T.Reardon and E. Youldon has also contributed some information. Sincere gratitude goes to all concerned.

GEOGRAPHICAL SETTING

Exeter is situated in the county of Devon on the River Exe which flows into the English Channel at Exmouth. Many sections of the Roman walls still remain intact and the tramways traversed these walls at various places.

The Ordnance Survey maps are to the scale of 25" to one mile and are of the horse tramway; unfortunately the electric tramway never appeared on the 25" maps as its opening and closure fell between survey dates.

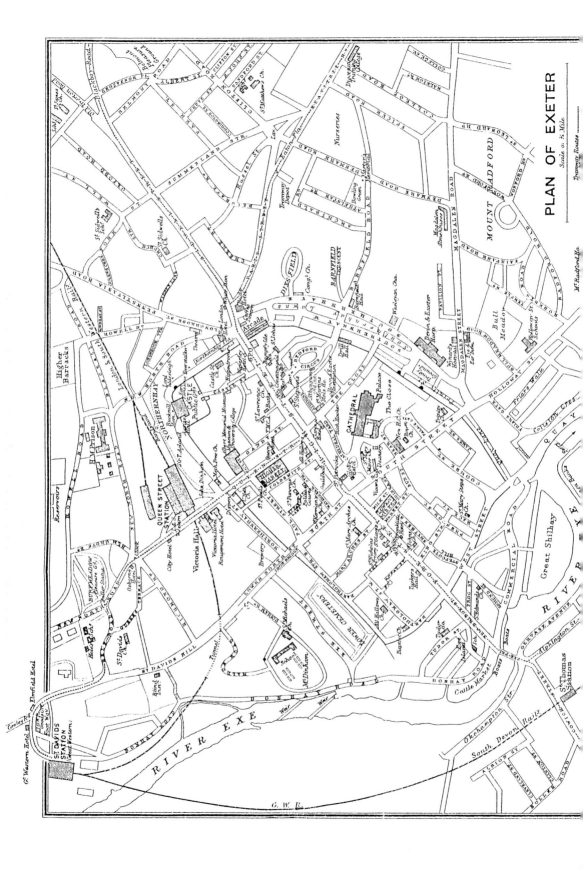

PLAN OF EXETER

Scale 0½ Mile

Tramway Routes

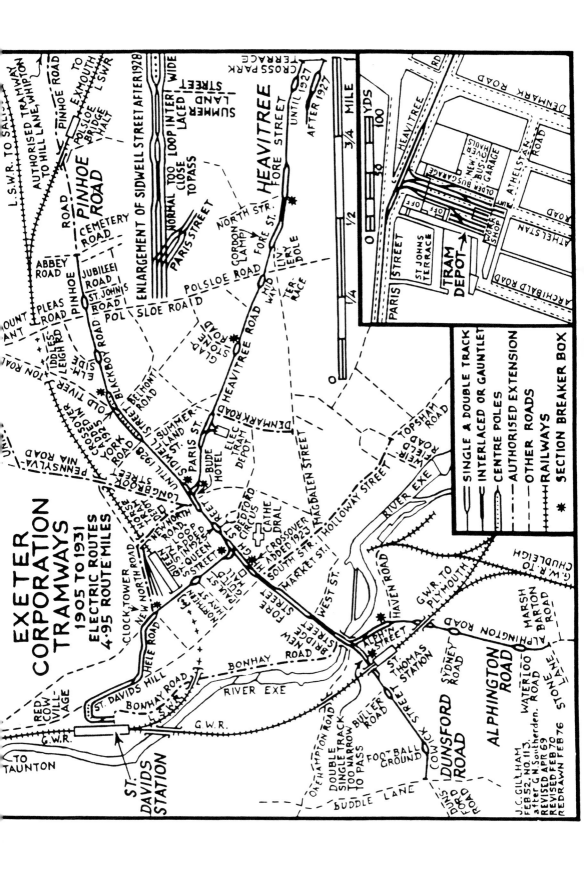

EXETER CORPORATION TRAMWAYS
1905 TO 1931
ELECTRIC ROUTES 4·95 ROUTE MILES

ENLARGEMENT OF SIDWELL STREET AFTER 1928

NORMAL TOO CLOSE LOOP INTERLACED TO PASS

SUMMERLAND STREET WIDE

PARIS STREET

NORTH STR.

HEAVITREE
FORE STREET

CROSS PARK TERRACE

UNTIL 1927

AFTER 1927

GORDON LAMP

FORE ST.

LIVERY DOLE

MID WAY TERRACE

POLSLOE ROAD

GLADSTONE ROAD

HEAVITREE ROAD

DENMARK ROAD

L.S.W.R. TO SALIS...

TO EXMOUTH L.S.W.R.

AUTHORISED TRAMWAY TO HILL LANE, WHIPTON

PINHOE ROAD

POLSLOE BRIDGE HALT

CEMETERY ROAD

PINHOE ROAD

ABBEY ROAD

JUBILEE ROAD

ST. JOHNS ROAD

PINHOE ROAD

POL SLOE ROAD

MOUNT PLEAS ANT ROAD

PENNSYLVA NIA ROAD

...TON ROAD

IDDLESLEIGH RD

ELM SIDE

BLACKBOY ROAD

BELMONT ROAD

OLD TIVER...

CROSSOVER YARDS 1928

A 492

YORK ROAD

LONGBROOK STREET UNTIL 1928

SIDWELL STREET

SUMMERLAND ST.

PARIS ST.

BUDE HOTEL

ELEC. TRAM DEPOT

DENMARK ROAD

MAGDALEN STREET

TOPSHAM ROAD

WEIRFIELD ROAD

RIVER EXE

HORSE TRAM DEPOT OLD

NEW NORTH ROAD

QUEEN LOOP ADDED IN 1925

QUEEN STREET

HIGH STREET

BEDFORD CIRCUS

CATHEDRAL

CROSSOVER ADDED 1923

SOUTH STR.

MARKET ST.

HOLLOWAY STREET

NEW NORTH ROAD

CLOCK TOWER

NORTH ST.

HAY ST.

FORE STREET

PAUL ST.

HIGH ST.

BRIDGE STREET

WEST ST.

NEW BRIDGE STREET

ALBERT STREET

HAVEN ROAD

G.W.R. TO PLYMOUTH

RIVER EXE

BONHAY ROAD

ST. DAVIDS HILL

BONHAY ROAD L.S.W.R.

RED COW VILLAGE

G.W.R.

TO TAUNTON

ST. DAVIDS STATION

G.W.R.

ST. THOMAS STATION

SYDNEY ROAD

ALPHINGTON ROAD

MARSH BARTON ROAD

WATERLOO ROAD

COWICK STREET

BUTLER ROAD

FOOT BALL GROUND

DUNSFORD ROAD

DOUBLE TRACK TOO NARROW SINGLE TRACK TO PASS

OKEHAMPTON ROAD

DUNS FORD ROAD

BUDDLE LANE

G.W.R. TO CHUDLEIGH

Legend

- ▭ SINGLE & DOUBLE TRACK
- ▭ INTERLACED OR GAUNTLET
- ● CENTRE POLES
- --- AUTHORISED EXTENSION
- --- OTHER ROADS
- +++ RAILWAYS
- * SECTION BREAKER BOX

Inset (Tram Depot)

DENMARK ROAD

HEAVITREE ... RD

ATHELSTAN ROAD

ARCHIBALD ROAD

PARIS STREET

ST JOHNS TERRACE

TRAM DEPOT

WORK SHOP

OLDER BUS GARAGE

NEW BUS GARAGE OVER HAULS

O   1/4   1/2   3/4 MILE
O   100   YDS

J.C.GILLHAM
FEB.52. NO.113.
after G.N.Southerden.
REVISED APR 69
REVISED FEB 70
REDRAWN FEB 76

HISTORICAL BACKGROUND

The name of the city is associated with the Romans who founded the settlement of Isca nearly two thousand years ago.

The cathedral was built in 1396 and in the High Street stands the Guildhall which is the oldest municipal building in the country and dates from 1492. A ship canal was constructed in 1566 between Topsham and the port of Exeter. The first railway to reach the city was the broad gauge (7ft/2133mm) Bristol and Exeter route which arrived at St. Davids station on 1st May 1844, whilst the rival standard gauge London & South Western reached Queen Street in July 1860.

Horse tramways operated from 1882 to 1905 on the following routes from London Inn Square: St.David's station via New North Road, Obelisk, Hele Road and St.David's Hill. Livery Dole via Paris Street and Heavitree Road. Mount Pleasant via Sidwell Street and Bath Road. Royal Albert Museum via Queen Street branch from the Obelisk. The depot was in New North Road. The track gauge was 3ft. 6ins./1067mm. and eight tramcars were supplied by the Bristol Wagon and Carriage Works Company in a livery of yellow and chocolate. The undertaking was sold to Exeter Corporation for £6,749 in 1904 and preparations then started for the new electric system which opened in the following year.

The electric routes were: Pinhoe Road, Sidwell Street, High Street, Exe Bridge and Alphington...Green disc indicator on a white background. Heavitree, Paris Street, High Street, Exe Bridge and Cowick Street...White cross on a red disc. Queen Street, Hele Road and St.David's station...White disc on a green background.

The corporation built a depot at the bottom of Paris Street and the facility continued to be used by motor buses until 1974. Traction current was supplied by the corporation power station at Haven Banks which opened in 1901. A new bridge was constructed over the River Exe in 1905 to accommodate the electric tramway and this structure survived until the late 1960s when it was replaced in connection with flood prevention works. The tram fleet numbered 37 vehicles, but there never was a car 13! The system settled down and performed a vital local service. However, motor buses were introduced on 1st April 1929 and from April 1930 no further heavy maintenance was undertaken to the tramways. The last car ran on 15th August 1931.

1. Opening of the electric tramways

1. Councillor E.C.Perry, Mayor of Exeter is at the controls of the opening special on 4th April 1905. (J.B.Perkin Coll.)

2. The procession reaches the Guildhall and here we see the Mayor addressing his fellow citizens from the top deck of the tram. (J.B.Perkin Coll.)

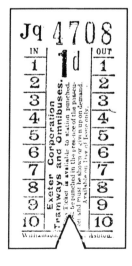

3. Car 19 is seen at the end of the track near St.David's station. Note that the indicator has already been turned for the city terminus in Queen Street. (G.N.Southerden)

4. This early panorama of the entrance to the station shows that the tramcar was the only motorised transport available to reach the city centre. (National Tramway Museum)

5. Car 17 is pictured here outside the Great Western Hotel in April 1926. Although the tram looks in good condition, it was scrapped shortly afterwards. (G.N.Southerden)

6. Car 10 battles up St.David's Hill in February 1929; in those days the service went on whatever the weather! (G.N.Southerden)

7. Track repairs by the clock tower and car 16 has been dewired to act as a waiting room for passengers transferring from shuttle car 7 seen in the background. (G.N.Southerden)

8. A well known local sight is the Jubilee Memorial Clock Tower at the end of Queen Street. Note the feeder wires for the traction current on the standard in the foreground. (J.B.Perkin Coll.)

9. Sometime later than the previous photo and car 3 now has the privilege of being a temporary waiting room as the track reconstruction makes progress down Queen Street. (G.N.Southerden)

10. This final view of the track works in Queen Street which was taken on 24th January 1929. (G.N.Southerden)

→

11. Car 12 has just crested the bridge at Queen Street station and is passing Peters and Hankins, Importers, at the corner of Northernhay Street. (National Tramway Museum)

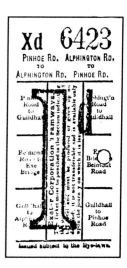

12. Note the splendid lamp standard in this photo of Queen Street in the first decade of the twentieth century. Car 10 makes its steady way northbound to St. David's station.
(R.J.Harley Coll.)

13. With journey's end in sight, car 15 reaches
the centre of the city. (G.N.Southerden)

14. The Royal Albert Memorial Museum
dominates Queen Street as a tramcar passes in
the sunshine. (National Tramway Museum)

15. In 1905 such was the demand for progress in municipal transport that most people would happily countenance the complete closure of High Street and Queen Street seen here in this picture, whilst tracks were laid for the modern marvel of electric traction.
(J.B.Perkin Coll.)

3. High Street - Alphington Road

16. The points leading to Queen Street can be seen clearly in this view of car 20 in the High Street. (National Tramway Museum)

17. Shortly after the opening of the system car 5 is caught by the camera as it passes the Guildhall on a short working to St.Thomas station. (National Tramway Museum)

18. This High Street scene dates from after World War I; the leading tram is heading for Cowick Street and Dunsford Road. (J.B.Perkin Coll.)

19. We take a last look at some of the fine architecture as car 18 passes on the Alphington route. (National Tramway Museum)

20. A very evocative scene from the tramway era as car 23 waits for sister car 28 to clear the interlaced track in Fore Street.
(G.N.Southerden)

21. We now reach Exe Bridge and observe car 1 emerging from Cowick Street in 1905. (J.B.Perkin Coll.)

22. Looking in the opposite direction to the previous photo, the brand new state of Exe Bridge can be appreciated with its ornate traction standards supporting the tramway overhead wires. (J.H.Price coll.)

23. This is the tram crash at Exe Bridge in 1917. Car 12 got out of control in Fore Street and hurtled towards the bridge where it overturned. A lady passenger was fatally injured and many others were treated for injuries and shock. The scene was captured by photographer Henry Wykes who quickly processed his plates and within one hour was selling postcards outside his studio nearby! (National Tramway Museum)

24. On 22nd, September 1906 the two trams shown here formed the opening convoy of the Alphington Road extension, which was the last new route in Exeter. This proved to be another popular event for Exonians.
(National Tramway Museum)

25. Twenty years further on at the same location featured in the previous view and car 27 is about to swing to the right of the picture. The trolley pole will then engage the hanging lever of the overhead line frog seen above the car; this will then switch the trolley wheel to the correct wire at the junction. (G.N.Southerden)

26. Further along Alphington Road car 10 pauses for the smart crew to have their photos taken. (R.J.Harley Coll.)

27. Sydney Street loop, Alphington Road, is the setting for car 29 which is waiting for another car to arrive from the city before it can proceed on its way. (G.N.Southerden)

Mw **6146**		
UP	**2d**	DOWN
Cross Park		Guil-hall
Tram Depot	Exeter Corporation Tramways. This ticket is available for the journey punched, must be punched in the presence of the passenger and must be retained, or given up on demand. It is available after passing one car, based subject to the Byelaws.	Duns-ford Rd
Top of Paris Street		Alphing-ton Road
1		1
2		2
PARCEL		
Williamson, Printer, Ashton.		

28. Again at the Sydney Street loop cars 2 and 27 pass. Although there is little other traffic, these single track and loop layouts could cause inconvenient waits for passengers and were one of the main reasons for replacement by motor buses. (G.N.Southerden)

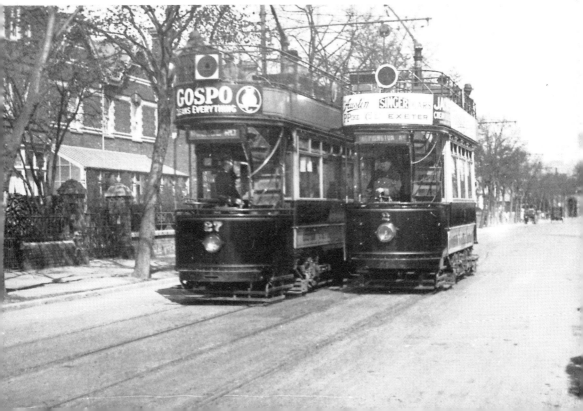

29. The terminus at Stone Lane with car 16 waiting to return across the city; note the crew member who is snatching a few moments rest before the off. (G.N.Southerden)

30. The date is June 1930 and three specials catering for greyhound racing enthusiasts are lined up at Stone Lane, Alphington Road terminus. The trams had a legendary capacity to swallow up sports crowds and cars would sometimes be groaning under the weight of fans with some riding on the fender! (G.N.Southerden)

4. Cowick Street

31. A study in light and shade as car 14 emerges from underneath the railway bridge at St. Thomas station. The station roof was designed by the famous engineer and visionary I.K. Brunel. (G.N.Southerden)

32. At the Falmouth Inn by Dunsford Road car 26 has reached the end of the track. The trolley pole has been turned as a couple of passengers run to catch the tram before the motorman gradually accelerates away. (G.N.Southerden)

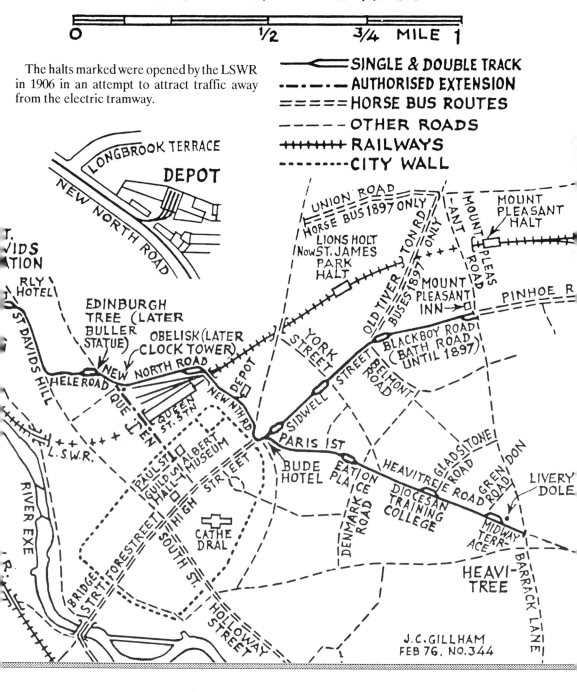

EXETER TRAMWAYS COMPANY
1882 TO 1905   HORSE TRAMWAYS
3'-6" GAUGE   2·34 ROUTE MILES

| 0 | ½ | ¾ | MILE | 1 |

The halts marked were opened by the LSWR in 1906 in an attempt to attract traffic away from the electric tramway.

SINGLE & DOUBLE TRACK
AUTHORISED EXTENSION
HORSE BUS ROUTES
OTHER ROADS
RAILWAYS
CITY WALL

J.C.GILLHAM
FEB 76. NO.344

33. At the junction of High Street, Paris Street and Sidwell Street two horse trams wait for the photographer before continuing to their respective suburban termini. (J.B.Perkin Coll.)

34. The sun is shining in Sidwell Street and an inspector talks to the motorman of car 6 as he waits for car 4 to clear the single line. In 1928 the track seen here was doubled to avoid this sort of delay. (J.B.Perkin Coll.)

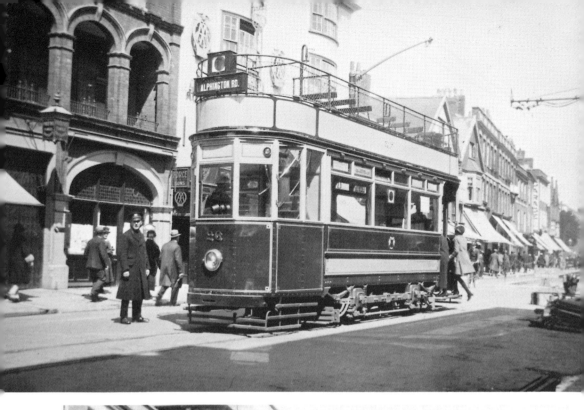

35. Car 26 waits in Sidwell Street as track repairs have cut the through service to Pinhoe Road. (G.N.Southerden)

37. Note the tracks in the foreground which were too close for cars to pass. One can only assume that this arrangement was adopted to save on points! Cars 1 and 4 stand on the loop outside St.Sidwell's Church. (G.N.Southerden)

36. These three cars were stored in Sidwell Street as track reconstruction had prevented their return from Pinhoe Road to the depot in Paris Street. (G.N.Southerden)

38. The horse trough at St.Sidwells plays host
to an assortment of vehicles including car 12.
Near this spot it is said that a hermit lived
before almshouses were erected in 1561.
(National Tramway Museum)

39. Another view of St.Sidwells shows part of a rather elegant centre standard with its wrought iron scroll work. This form of traction standard could be found in Exeter outside the Great Western Hotel and here in Sidwell Street between York Road and Belmont Road. (J.B.Perkin Coll.)

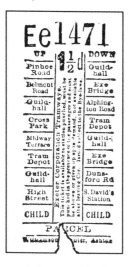

40. More special cars, this time laid on for football fans. The trams are seen here near Belmont Road. (G.N.Southerden)

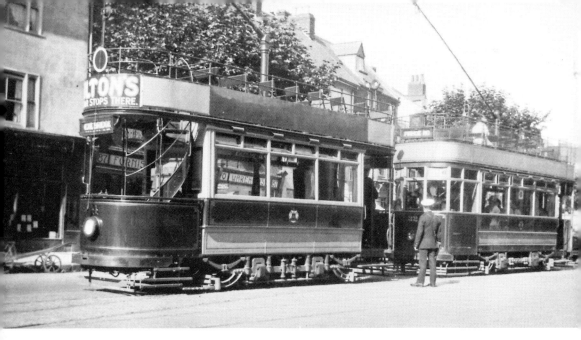

41. Car 11 has open platforms whilst car 32 in front is of a more modern design with platform vestibules which gave protection for the crew in inclement weather. These two trams were captured on film at Belmont Road on 17th September 1927. (G.N.Southerden)

42. The conductor turns towards the photographer as car 26 is caught in time near the Pinhoe Road terminus at Abbey Road. (G.N.Southerden)

6. Paris Street - Depot - Heavitree

43. Near the depot in Paris Street car 32 is seen passing a delivery van. Notice the 18 inch margin of granite setts on the outside of the double track which according to law every tramway operator had to maintain for all road users. (J.B.Perkin Coll.)

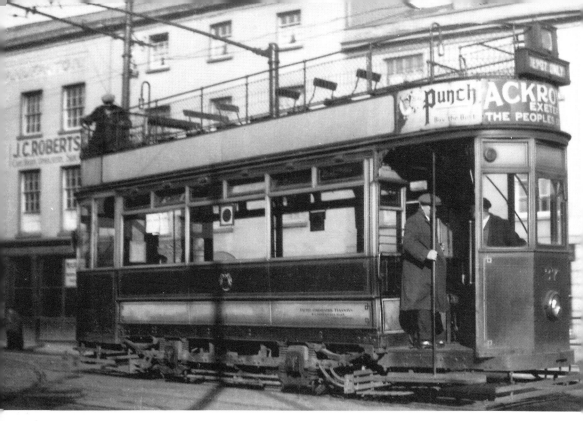

44. The tramway maintenance staff are on board car 27 which has just emerged from the depot for a test run before entering normal service. (G.N.Southerden)

← ———————

45. Opposite the depot and a car with an empty top deck comes to a halt. Note that some of the seats "outside" are not all facing the same way; normally it was the conductor's duty to see that all passengers faced the direction of travel. (G.N.Southerden)

46. Further running repairs are carried out while the passengers wait patiently. Actually the trams were very reliable and would always get you through even in the worst snow and fog. (G.N.Southerden)

——————— →

47. There was a nice style to the entrance of the Paris Sreet depot and the building reflects the turn of the century municipal pride in providing elegant structures for important public utilities. (G.N.Southerden)

Overleaf →
48. Inside the depot the trams could be moved over inspection pits so that repairs to trucks, brakes and motors could be effected. Although space is at a premium, everything seems to fit in neatly. (G.N.Southerden)

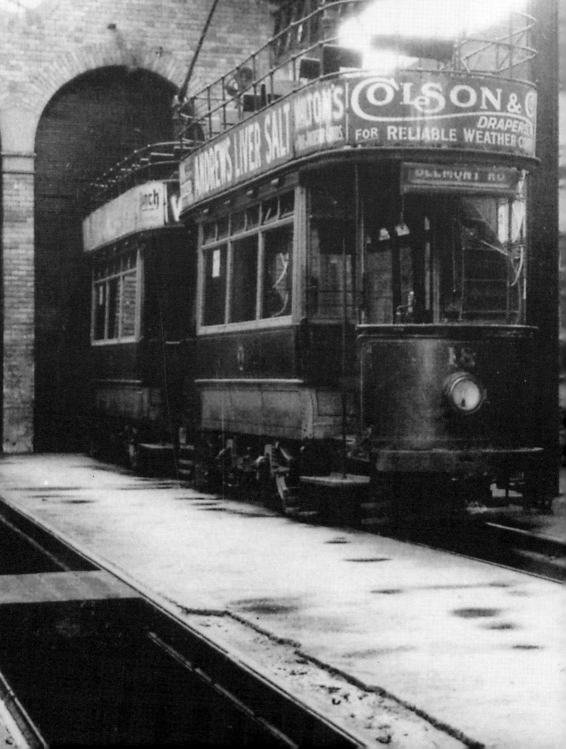

49. It must have been a big moment for the aspiring schoolboy driver, perhaps he was related to one of the staff pictured here. (National Tramway Museum)

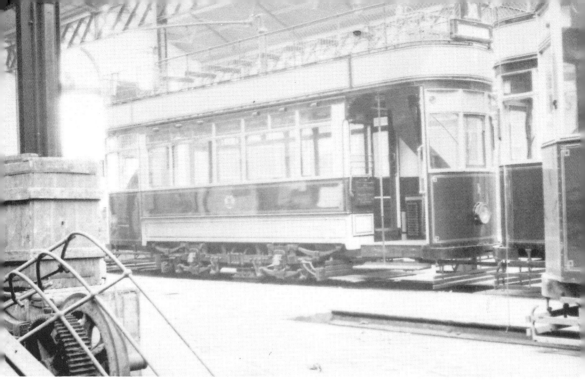

50. The new car 1 positively gleams on one of the depot roads; it arrived in Exeter in 1929. Less encouraging in the foreground is evidence that at least one former inmate has been recently broken up. (G.N.Southerden)

51. The loop at Midway Terrace by the former Livery Dole horse tram terminus was a favourite spot for local photographer G.N. Southerden. Here car 22 has just stopped to let a passenger alight. (G.N.Southerden)

52. The motorman of car 25 turns to peer in
the lower saloon as he waits at Midway Terrace
loop. (G.N.Southerden)

53. A lone motorcyclist approaches and car 32 loads passengers before leaving Midway Terrace. (G.N.Southerden)

54. In 1927 track repairs interrupted the through service to Heavitree; car 4 is stationed on the city side of the road works awaiting transfer passengers. (G.N.Southerden)

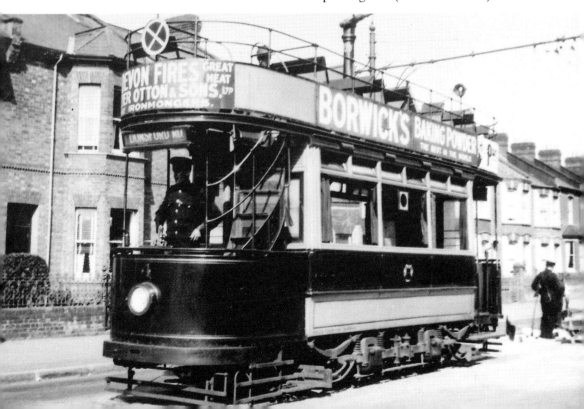

55. Track relaying at Butts Road continues;
car 20 stands devoid of passengers and crew.
(G.N.Southerden)

56. Heavitree terminus and the crew stand
proudly by their vehicle. The lack of traffic in
those days is in stark contrast to today's
congestion and exhaust fumes.
(G.N.Southerden)

57. The horse era of tramway operation on Heavitree Road is marked by this view of an Exeter Tramways Co. car bearing an advert for the unfortunately named St.Erile mineral water! (J.B.Perkin Coll.)

58. The last car on Heavitree Road is driven by Mr E.C.Perry who was mayor at the time of the opening (see picture no. 1). The date is 19th August 1931 and a replacment bus is bring up the rear. (J.B.Perkin Coll.)

7. Rolling Stock

The fleet of Exeter Corporation Tramways consisted of traditional British four wheel open top cars. Many trams were fitted with platform vestibules and new dashes which gave them a more modern appearance. Livery was originally dark green and cream, with gold lettering shaded pink. The truck sides were painted green, but the rest of the undergear remained dark maroon. From March 1925 a lighter "Napier" green became the standard and the gold lettering on the rocker panels was left off.

CARS 1-12. Built at Preston in 1905, they rode on Brill 21E trucks and seated 20 in the lower saloon and 22 on the top deck. **Cars 2, 3 and 4** were renumbered 5, 7 and 19 respectively in 1929. Car 12 was withdrawn after the Exe Bridge accident in 1917 and its usable parts were cannibalised to keep other cars running!

CARS 14-15. Built at Preston in 1905, these two trams were very similar to the original batch. Car 14 was the last Exeter tram and closed the system in 1931.

CARS 16-21. Built at Preston in 1906 in the standard Exeter four wheel open top design. Car 19 received platform vestibules and a new dash around 1926; it was renumbered 21 in 1929. In the same year car 21 was renumbered 17.

CARS 22-25. Built by Brush in 1914, these cars were slightly longer than their predecessors and they seated 24 on the top deck. They were fitted with Brill 21E trucks. Cars 22-24 were given platform vestibules around 1926.

CARS 26-27. Built by Brush in 1921 on Peckham long wheelbase P22 trucks. They seated 30 on the top deck and later received platform vestibules with new angular dashes.

CARS 28-30. Built by Brush in 1925 and equipped with 7ft. wheelbase Brill 21E trucks, these cars were delivered with platform vestibules.

CARS 31-34. Built by Brush in 1926, they were identical to the 1925 cars.

CARS 1-4.(SECOND SERIES) Built by Brush in 1929, these cars ran on Peckham P35 trucks and they were delivered with platform vestibules. They were the last new cars to be built for any West Country system and they had a very short life in Exeter.

After abandonment, cars 26-34 were sold to Plymouth, being renumbered in their fleet, 8, 9, and 1-7 respectively. Exeter cars 1-4 (second series) were sold to Halifax and became cars 128-131 in the Yorkshire town's fleet.

59. Here we see one of the original trams from the 1-12 batch. Note the folding lattice gate with which the motorman could close the driving platform. (J.B.Perkin Coll.)

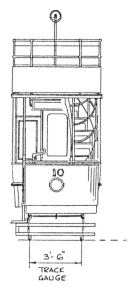

3'- 6"
TRACK
GAUGE

60. Smartly turned out with curtains at the lower saloon windows, a car is pictured shortly before the service opened. (National Tramway Museum)

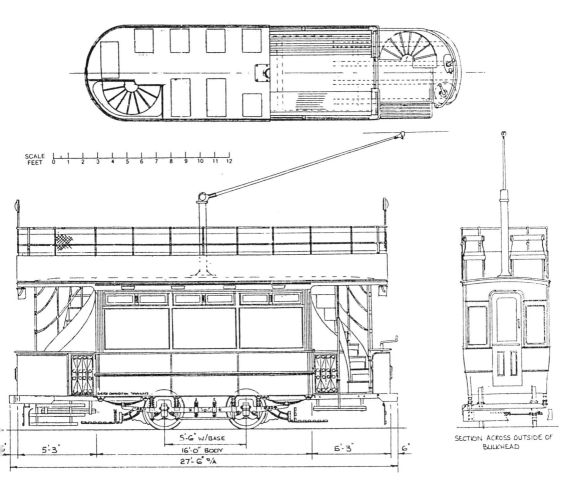

SCALE FEET 0 1 2 3 4 5 6 7 8 9 10 11 12

5'-3"
5'-6" W/BASE
16'-0" BODY
27'-6" O/A
6'-3"
6'

SECTION ACROSS OUTSIDE OF BULKHEAD

61. One of the early cars is seen in original livery with the band neatly ensconced on the top deck. (C.Carter)

62. Car 19 received a new platform vestibule and angular dashes in the middle 1920s. The livery has been changed to a lighter green and the lettering on the rocker panels of the tram has been omitted. (G.N.Southerden)

63. Car 22 was built by Brush in 1914 and it is shown in its original condition, but in the second livery in 1926. (G.N.Southerden)

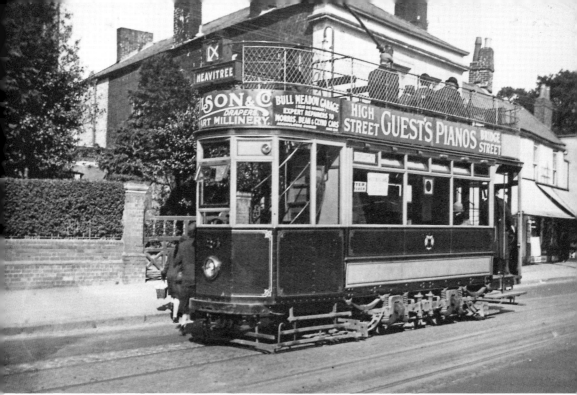

64. In its rebuilt state car 24 shows clearly the platform vestibule which has been added, plus the new angular dash plate.
(G.N.Southerden)

←——————

65. An end on view of car 30 which was supplied to the corporation in 1925 already fitted with platform vestibules.
(National Tramway Museum)

——————→

67. The second series of cars 1-4 had a very odd lower saloon window arrangement.
(G.N.Southerden)

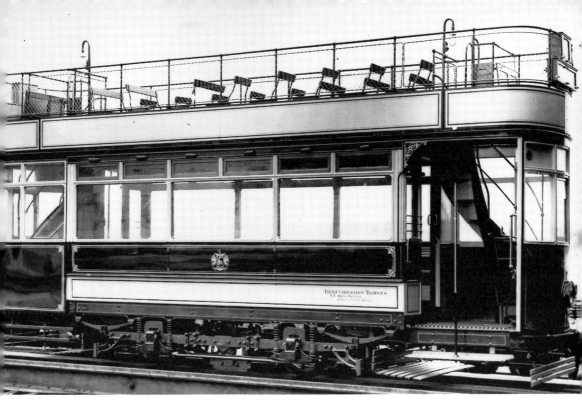

66. Cars 31-34 were splendid vehicles, if a little outdated by retaining open tops. The "powers that be" in Whitehall were always somewhat reluctant to allow four wheel covered top cars on narrow gauge systems, the thinking being that they were more unstable in accidents and high winds than eight wheel enclosed cars or vehicles running on wider standard gauge tracks. (National Tramway Museum)

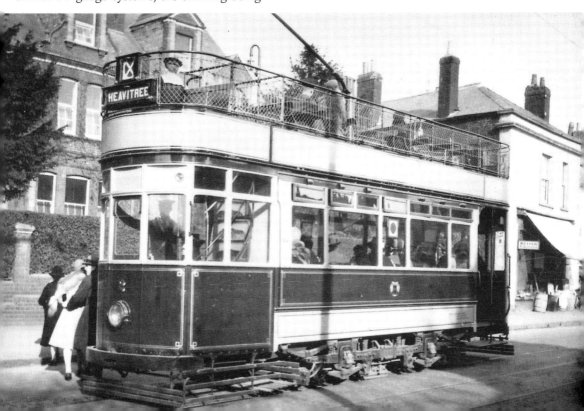

68. Car 7 was stripped of its staircase and kitted out as a snow plough. Note the bulkhead door which has been slid open.
(G.N.Southerden)

69. At the end of Exeter tramways in 1931 several cars migrated northwards to the West Yorkshire town of Halifax. Here is a vehicle from the Exeter second series cars 1-4 with its new owners. (N.Kirk)

70. Some Exeter cars stayed in their home county and gave a few more years service in Plymouth. (R.J.Harley Coll.)

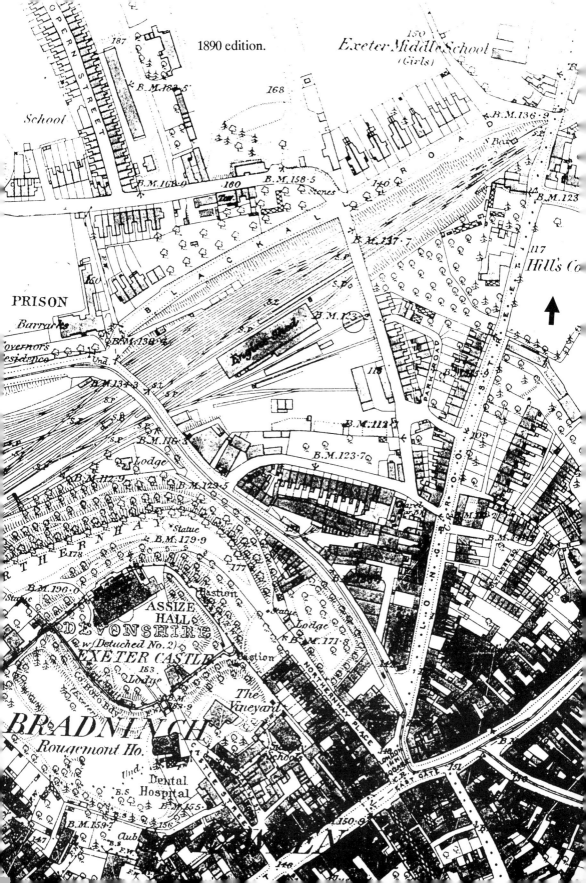

TAUNTON TRAMWAYS

CONTENTS PART 2

INTRODUCTION

In 1986 I was requested by my employer to organise an exhibition in Taunton Library to celebrate the centenary of electric street lighting in the town. I also arranged for the manufacture and erection of a reproduction arc lamp and column on The Parade. This was switched on by the then Mayor with the Christmas tree lights for the 1986 season's decorations. During my investigations I came across a large amount of information on the Taunton electric tramways; the history of electric lighting, traction and generation, usually direct current, was closely interwoven at the turn of the twentieth century.

Thus was commenced the quest for a fuller knowledge of the history of the tramways in Taunton. Some gaps remain to be filled and it is hoped that readers may be able to locate photographs of the original and later northern termini; track laying, repair and removal; and finally two trams at a passing loop. Provided I can raise the necessary sponsorship, it is hoped to produce a larger format publication in 2001 to mark the centenary of the opening of the tramway. I will also require the services of a local artist who can capture the colour and flavour of the Taunton street scene at the beginning of this century.

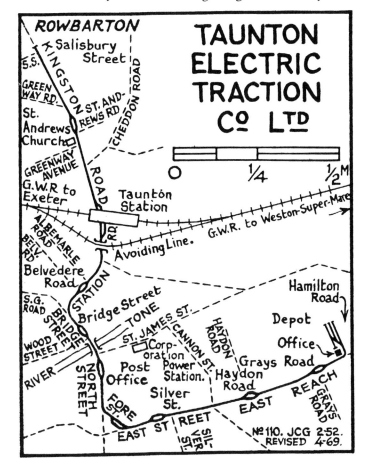

GEOGRAPHICAL SETTING

Taunton is the administative centre of the county of Somerset, it lies on the River Tone which flows through the Vale of Taunton Deane. The town is surrounded by some attractive countryside including the Quantock and Blackdown Hills. In 1921 the population of the town was 23,223.

The maps are from the 1914 edition Ordnance Survey and are to the scale of 25" to 1 mile.

HISTORICAL BACKGOUND

A castle was first built in the area in about 710 by the West Saxon King Ine. Many centuries later it was the site of the so called "Bloody Assizes" conducted by Judge Jeffrys after the ill fated rebellion of the Duke of Monmouth in 1685. The Bristol and Exeter Railway reached Taunton on 1st July 1842 and this event is celebrated by a plaque erected by Taunton Deane Borough Council in 1985. Further branch lines followed to Chard, Barnstaple and Minehead.

The town attracted the attention of the powerful British Electric Traction group and a company was incorporated in 1900 with the title of Taunton and West Somerset Electric Railways and Tramways Co.. There were big plans to establish a tramway network radiating from the county town, however, the reality was different and what followed was the construction of the smallest urban electric tramway in Great Britain! Opened in August 1901 it was just over a mile long with eight passing places; the track gauge was 3ft. 6ins/1067mm., the maximum gradient 1 in 25 and the sharpest curve had a radius of 35ft. The name of the undertaking was changed to the more realistic Taunton Electric Traction Co.

and all vehicles carried the BET Company's "wheel and magnet" insignia. Relaying of the whole system took place in 1905 and the service ceased for two months, during which time the original fleet of six open top cars was sold to Leamington and Warwick Tramways Co.; six replacement single deck cars were ordered for the line. The only extension was opened on 13th August 1909 from the original terminus at the railway station to a new one at the junction of Kingston Road with Salisbury Street, Rowbarton. At its full extent from 1909-1921 the tramway was just under one and a half miles in length with ten passing loops and a depot situated at the terminus of East Reach.

After World War I it became clear that the system's prospects were not good and following a dispute with Taunton Corporation over the price of traction current, the power supply was switched off and service ceased on 28th May 1921. An offer by the BET to sell the undertaking to the corporation for £7000 was turned down due to the precarious financial state of the tramway. The six tramcars were all sold, three going to Torquay, two to Gravesend in Kent and one became a garden shed!

8. Depot Shed - East Reach

71. Inside the depot at the start of operations in 1901, we see a group of staff including B.H. Griffith on the left of the front row and Robert Croker is standing far right. (R.J.Croker)

72. W.Smith, the Manager, his wife and daughter are glimpsed on the top deck of car 5 probably in 1905 before the trams were dismantled for transport to Leamington. The dash of the tram has suffered during four years service. (National Tramway Museum)

73. Interior of the tram sheds with the rails and inspection pits in situ in 1983. Note the narrow gauge of the track. A section of rail was presented to the school museum service in Staplegrove Road and the author has arranged for this to be shot blasted. (V.V.Verrier)

74. Single deck car 6 has just been delivered from Brush in Loughborough to the depot in East Reach. The date is 1905 and B.H.Griffith is on the left. (National Tramway Museum)

75. Three single deck cars act as backdrop to
this staff group assembled outside the depot.
(R.J.Croker)

76. Note the passengers in the car although the official stop was in East Reach. The overhead repair wagon is in the background. The tram is liberally plastered with advertisements and the name of Hawkes continues today as Hawkes Oils Ltd. (National Tramway Museum)

77. One of the single deck cars photographed outside the depot with the overhead repair wagon. This wagon is seen later in Kingston Road. Note the "home made" access platform on top of the car. (Somerset County Council)

78. George Townsend, Bob Croker, Freddie
Everard and Bill Benginfield are on the overhead inspection platform perched on one of
the single deck cars. (R.J.Croker)

79. The entrance track to the depot seen here in 1910 was the sharpest curve on the system; it entered a narrow unmade lane at the turning after Alfred Street. At the sheds (measuring 120ft. by 35ft.) the line fanned out into three roads. The manager's house is at the left of the depot entrance; today the house to the right is the Night Shelter with the Leper Hospital of St.Margaret, recently damaged by fire, in the background. (N.Chipchase Coll.)

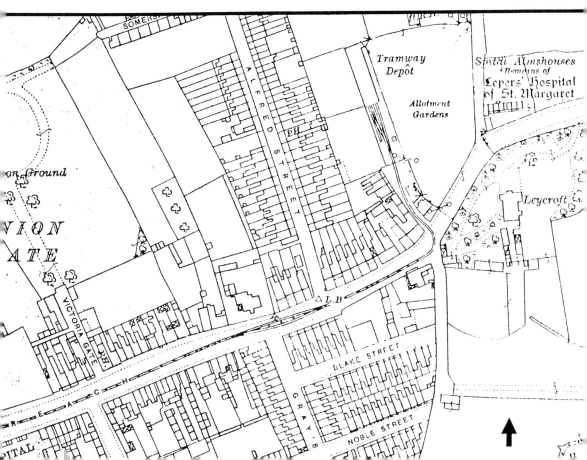

80. Car 4 is pictured at the East Reach terminus; this spot is close to the present day traffic signals by the high mast at the southern end of Victoria Parkway.
(National Tramway Museum)

81. Note the pristine condition of car 1 about to make its first run in 1905; the state of the car without disfiguring advertisements can be appreciated. (A.J.Watkin coll.)

82. Double deck car 1 is eastbound in East Reach when a boy could stand in the road with no fear of the traffic. The highway has just been watered on both sides to lay the dust of a high summer long ago.
(National Tramway Museum)

83. The overhead power supply is visible at the corner of Tancred Street and East Reach. (J.H.Price coll.)

9. East Street - Fore Street

84. We now arrive at East Street in company with car 1 as it wends its way eastbound past the horse bus outside Claridge's London Hotel (now the County Hotel). The ground floor of the building in the centre of the scene is now the AA insurance office. The shop canopy supports were ideal for tethering horses or propping up bicycles. (J.B.Perkin Coll.)

85. This group of children is gathered outside
the London Hotel run by Ernest Claridge; the
view dates from around 1909.
(National Tramway Museum)

86. A view of East Street in 1914 is included to
show the layout of the track and the part of the
setted roadway for which the tramway company
had maintenance responsibility. Montague
Cooper's photography studio "Acacia House" is
on the extreme right.
(National Tramway Museum)

87. A passenger alights from a single deck car waiting at the Fore Street loop around 1909. Note the arches of the Market House which were removed in the 1930s for road widening. The long bracket arm supporting the overhead wires is also worthy of note. (National Tramway Museum)

88. An eastbound car halts at Fore Street loop. The Market House is decorated with posters for horse and dog shows. (National Tramway Museum)

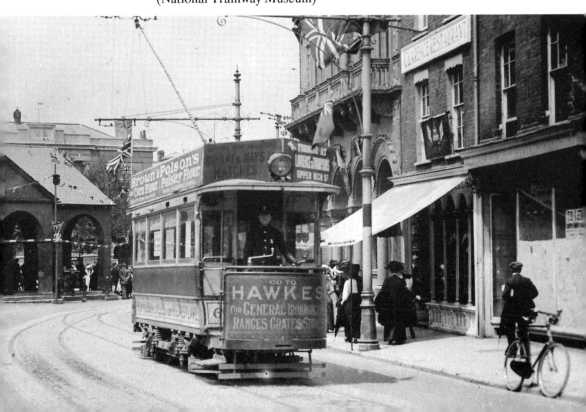

89. The attractive scroll work on the traction standard can be noted; it is hoped to reproduce some of this work for the centenary in 2001. (National Tramway Museum)

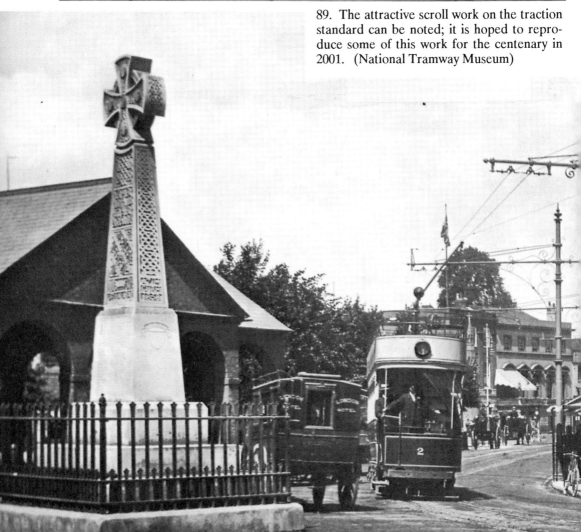

91. Car 3 passes Hammet Street on its way to the Station Road terminus in 1902. The attractive building on the corner of Hammet Street and Fore Street gave way to the 1960s Lloyds building. (A.Fiveash)

90. In Fore Street car 2 is about to pass a horse bus and the Burma War Memorial. (J.B.Perkin Coll.)

92. A southbound double deck car passes Hammet Street opposite the Parade in Fore Street. North Street is in the distance with the Castle Hotel behind the tram. Note the condition of the road and the old man pushing a hand delivery cart.
(Somerset County Council)

93. Car 3 is northbound in Fore Street heading towards the railway station; the three bollards in the left foreground protect the Parade.
(National Tramway Museum)

94. At the Kinglake Memorial a single deck car passes northbound. The highly ornate cast iron columns on the Parade gave way to a plainer art nouveau style in the early 1920s. (J.B.Perkin Coll.)

95. A relatively busy traffic scene with Great Western Railway horse drawn delivery vehicles in the left foreground; note that the arc lamp has duplicated luminaires, probably because of their unreliability. (Taunton Deane Borough Council.)

96. Car 1 heads northwards past the Castle
Hotel on the left and Westminster House on
the right. (J.B.Perkin Coll.)

97. North Street in 1902 with a boy and a calf   on the right is for milk delivery.
in front of the Castle Hotel; note the portico   (J.B.Perkin Coll.)
entrance over the footpath. The unusual cart

98. Another view taken in 1902 with only horse drawn traffic and bicycles present. The column to the left of this picture was used to prepare drawings for the reproduction arc lamp in 1986. (J.B.Perkin Coll.)

99. Opening day on 21st August 1901 and the decorated tramcar is positioned in North Street at around 5pm; two cars were decorated by W&A Chapman Ltd. and an estimated 2000 people had rides during the evening. (Montague Cooper Studio)

100. Motor traffic is beginning to compete for road space and the approaching motorist is quite happy to flout the highway code. This sort of conduct was dangerous for passengers who had to alight from the trams at some distance from the kerb. Note the Post Office clock just visible behind the tram; this building was opened in 1911 on the site of the former "Spread Eagle Inn" closed by the temperance movement. (National Tramway Museum)

101. Single deck car 6 is travelling north towards Chapmans department store. Again the nearer cyclist makes no attempt to keep to the left. (National Tramway Museum)

102. A southbound double deck tram crosses Tone Bridge whilst an oarsman rows upstream perhaps towards French Weir. (National Tramway Museum)

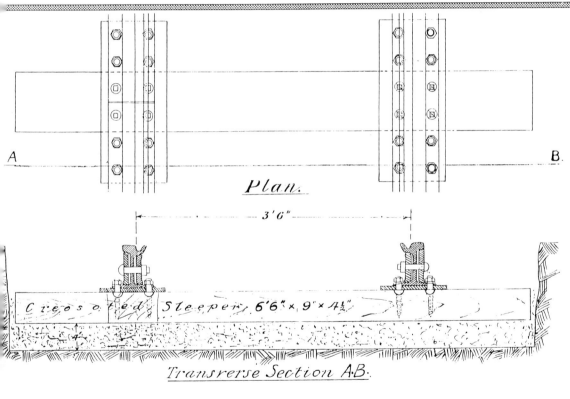

Plan.

3'6"

Creosoted Sleeper, 6'6" × 9" × 4½"

Transverse Section A·B.

Concrete.   *Concrete.*

Longitudinal Section

103. At Bridge Street loop a car waits sometime before the cinema was built in 1913.
Winters ironmongers shop on the left was later
demolished to widen Wood Street.
(National Tramway Museum)

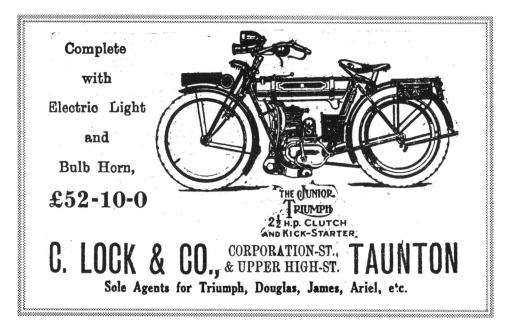

11. Station Road - Kingston Road

104. The old George Inn was demolished in 1907 and is now the site of the cinema. Flook House, then a private residence, is visible over the wall on the left hand side of Station Road. The fire department's emergency ladder was kept by the double arc lamp.
(National Tramway Museum)

105. Although the motorman is stationed as though the car is about to set off south, the trolley is facing in the opposite direction! This posed view has the wall of Flook House on the left. The road at this point is now considerably wider with a terrace of shops on the right. (National Tramway Museum)

106. Car 4 passes the narrow entrance to Canal Road. The posters advertise Buffalo Bill's Wild West Show which arrived in Taunton in August of 1903. Note the conductor collecting fares on the top deck. (National Tramway Museum)

107. In sight of the first terminus just beyond the railway bridge loop, a tram has the road to itself. (N.Chipchase Coll.)

108. Still in Station Road, a single deck car carries advertisements for Hawkes and a well known green and white one for Lipton's Tea. (National Tramway Museum)

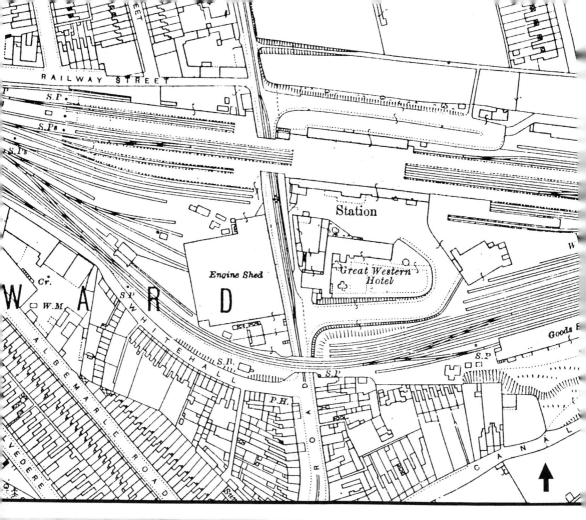

109. We reach the end of the line in Kingston Road, quite literally in this case as the tower wagon is being used to aid the dismantling of the overhead wires. The track has already been lifted. (N.Chipchase Coll.)

12. Power Supply

110. Following closure of the tramways the traction standards continued to be used as street lamp supports both in situ and relocated at other sites. Nine standards still exist in Greenway Crescent, the base of one of which is seen here restored to its former glory with the BET "wheel and magnet" device picked out in gold. This photo was taken in the spring of 1993. A tenth tramway standard is to be found in Bishops Lydeard.
(Taunton Deane Borough Council)

111. A couple of the DC generators feature here at St.James Street power station.
(SW Electric Plc.)

13. Rolling Stock

112. Car 1 has been jacked up and the truck removed in preparation for the transfer to Leamington in 1905. (National Tramway Museum)

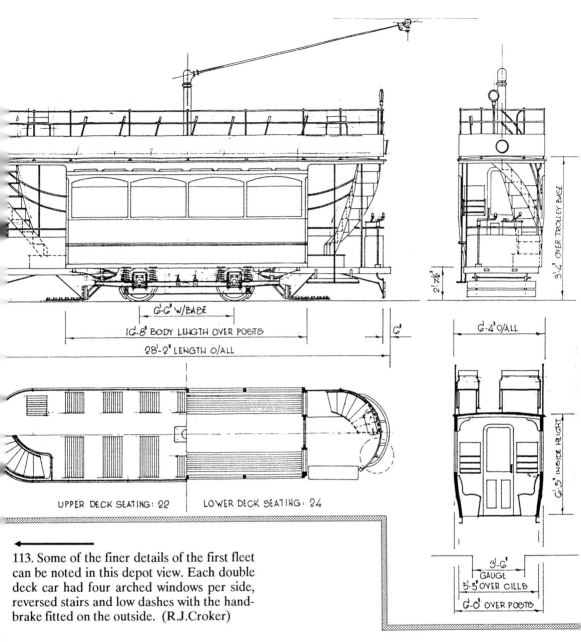

Figure labels:

- 6'-6" W/BASE
- 16'-8" BODY LENGTH OVER POSTS
- 28'-2" LENGTH O/ALL
- 6'
- UPPER DECK SEATING: 22
- LOWER DECK SEATING: 24
- 9'-4" OVER TROLLEY BASE
- 2'-7½"
- 6'-4" O/ALL
- 6'-5" INSIDE HEIGHT
- 3'-6" GAUGE
- 5'-5" OVER CILLS
- 6'-0" OVER POSTS

113. Some of the finer details of the first fleet can be noted in this depot view. Each double deck car had four arched windows per side, reversed stairs and low dashes with the handbrake fitted on the outside. (R.J.Croker)

Taunton was unusual in that it experienced a complete fleet renewal just four years after opening; six double deck cars were replaced with an equal number of single deck cars in 1905. Obviously passenger loading expectations were set rather too high at the inauguration of the service. Livery of the trams was crimson lake and cream with the fleet number gold shaded black; the BET "wheel and magnet" on the waist panel of each car was in gold with the "sparks" shaded appropriately electric blue!

CARS 1-5. Built by Brush in 1901, these trams were open top four wheel cars on Brush A1

trucks. They seated 22 in the lower saloon and 29 on the top deck.

CAR 6. Built by Brush in 1902 and identical to the previous batch.

All six double deck cars were sold to Leamington and Warwick Tramways in 1905.

CARS 1-6. (SECOND SERIES) These were single deck cars built by Brush in 1905 and placed on Brush A1 trucks; they each had a seating capacity of 24.

In 1921 five cars were sold; two went to Gravesend, becoming cars 7 and 8 in that fleet. Three trams became Torquay cars 34-36.

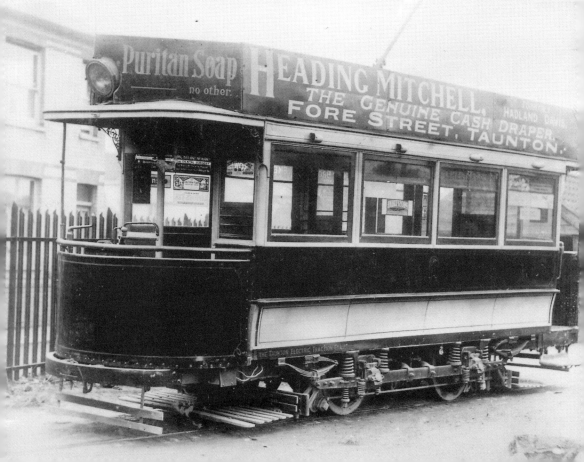

114. The single deck cars had a short central section enclosed by bulkhead doors; on either side was a further section one window in length where smoking was allowed. (Mrs.W.J.Yard)

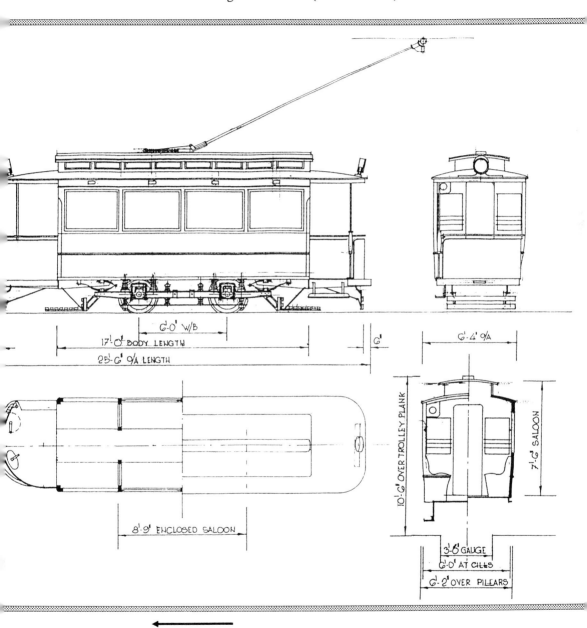

115. After advertisements were applied to each car, the fleet numbers were not visible but the staff could still recognise each car. (National Tramway Museum)

14. Finale

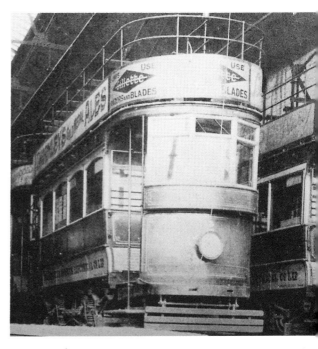

116. The poster reads "ride now, next week will be too late" in this photo that was taken at the time of the last run in late May 1921. (R.J.Croker)

117. The body of car 1 was placed on a trailer and towed around town by a steam traction engine. Here is the festive duo at the 1921 carnival. The placard on the roof of the car is a parody of the hit song of the period "Yes, We Have No Bananas!" (N.Chipchase Coll.)

118. Leamington and Warwick car 2 in November 1929, fully 24 years after leaving Taunton. Note that it has been fitted with a rather ugly windscreen; the car survived until 1930. (G.N.Southerden)

119. A glimpse of two of the ex-Taunton single deck cars in service at Torquay. The local tramway company altered the platform dashes for one man operation. The cars normally worked in summer only on the Torre Station to St.Marychurch route. (G.N.Southerden)

120. Gravesend and Northfleet car 7 is also a refugee from Somerset and on arrival in North Kent it was regauged to run on the standard (4ft. 8½ins./1435mm.) Gravesend tracks. The platforms have also been altered for one man operation; this tramway was replaced by buses in 1929. (R.J.Harley Coll.)

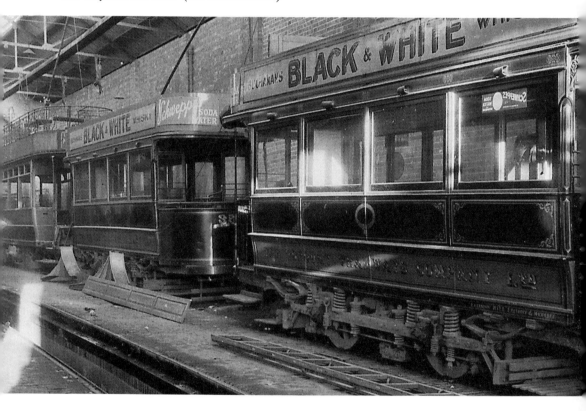

121. In 1992-93 the West Somerset Railway commissioned 7mm scale models of the double deck and single deck Taunton cars for their proposed visitor's centre. The models were constructed by Geof. Sawford of the Seaton Tramway in Devon. (J.B.Perkin)

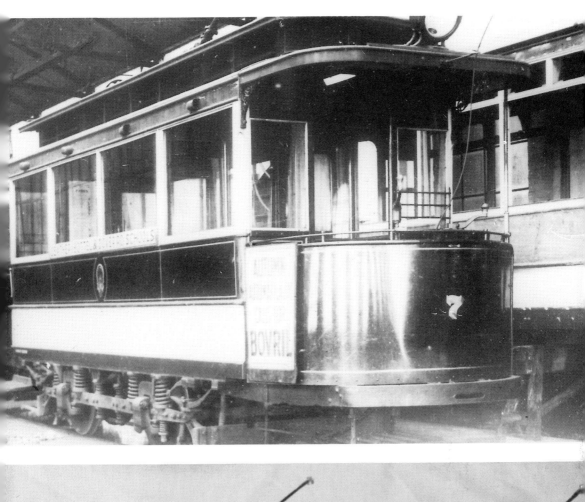